LOVE

PEACE

PATIENCE

KINDNESS

GOODNESS

FAITHFULNESS

JOY

GENTLENESS

SELFCONTROL

God has a plan for

_____

_____

_____

The plans of the LORD
stand firm forever,
the purposes of his heart
through all generations.

PSALM 33:11

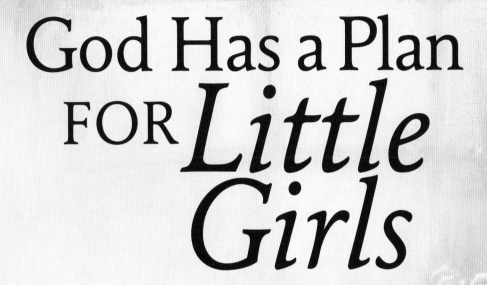

God Has a Plan
FOR *Little*
Girls

PAINTINGS BY

Kathryn Andrews Fincher

Text by Janna Walkup

HARVEST HOUSE PUBLISHERS

EUGENE, OREGON

God Has a Plan for Little Girls
Artwork Copyright © 2008 by Kathryn Andrews Fincher
Text Copyright © 2008 by Harvest House Publishers
Published by Harvest House Publishers
Eugene, OR 97402
www.harvesthousepublishers.com

ISBN-13: 978-0-7369-2151-0
ISBN-10: 0-7369-2151-6

Design and production by Koechel Peterson & Associates, Inc.,
Minneapolis, Minnesota

Printed in Thailand

08 09 10 11 12 13 / IM / 10 9 8 7 6 5 4 3 2

This book is dedicated to author and speaker Kay Arthur. Kay and I are not relatives or even close personal friends. However, Kay followed God's call and wrote a powerful Bible study that reached out to me and changed my heart. Like ripples from a drop of water, one person's faith and obedience spread out, and they have the power to change other people's lives. Through Kay's study on marriage, I was convicted to let go of my selfishness and focus on motherhood, and the love that overflowed became my palette.

I also dedicate this book to all the young readers who feel a stirring in their own hearts and seek to know God's plan for their lives. ✳

Many, O Lord my God,

are the wonders you have done.

The things you planned for

no one can recount to you;

were I to speak and tell of them,

they would be too many to declare.

PSALM 40:5

4

INTRODUCTION

When I was just three years old, I came upon an open can of green house paint that inspired me to try my hand at painting. But what would I paint? Aha! My four-year-old brother! My parents made sure I never created a work of art like *that* again, but the artist in me had been awakened. I drew stick figures, sketched page after page of horses, and experimented with oils to create wildlife scenes. I left trails of sketches throughout the house, but I never really thought God had a plan for me to be an artist!

Soon, I fell in love with sports. I remember the first time I stood up on water skis. I was hooked! I skied all year long—waterskiing in the summers, snow skiing in the winters. The more I skied, the better I got. Eventually, I was performing in water ski shows and even became a national water ski champion. I loved how God had given me the talent for such a fun activity.

When I married my husband, Jef, I didn't plan to have children. I wanted to keep competing in sports. But God had a different plan. I became pregnant, and little Maggie entered our life. And then little Kelley came along. *God, what is Your plan for me now?* I wondered. *I want to keep skiing, but how can I do that and be a mom at the same time?*

My husband and I took a study by a Bible teacher named Kay Arthur. Through this study, I realized that God had made me especially for the job of being my girls' mother. So, as I had throughout my life, I surrendered to God and allowed Him to guide me. *You know me better than I know myself, Lord,* I prayed. *I love You enough to give up my skiing, and I trust You for my future. Please show me the way.*

Soon, God made it clear that I was to return to the love of my childhood—painting. Using my own daughters and neighbor children as my models, I began to create pictures that told stories and showed people that children just like you are precious gifts from God.

When I was 9 years old, I gave my heart to Jesus. In my excitement about my faith, I grew up dreaming that God had some BIG amazing deed that He was planning for me that would CHANGE THE WORLD! I couldn't wait! Maybe you feel that way too. What I've discovered is that it didn't really happen for me that way. My faith and I grew up together, with one small step of faith daily. Today God has given me an important job of serving Him in some BIG ways, like creating this book. Yet, it was the small steps that brought me here.

As you read about the young years of these heroes that God calls to follow His plan, you will discover that what each one does as a child matters. And what you do matters too! Why? Because each small step of faith will prepare you for God's call.

For God has a plan...especially for you! ✳

Kathy Fincher

An Obedient Heart

*Blessed rather are those who hear
the word of God and obey it.*

· LUKE 11:28

S HE WAS JUST a simple village girl, devout in her faith and obedient to her parents. Her background was nothing special—her mother and father were loving, to be sure, yet the family had no wealth or position. Their small home was nestled in the hills, a pleasing place yet without the excitement and adventure of the city.

Nurtured by her parents and the local religious leaders, she learned to follow the laws of her faith diligently and without question. Obedient in spirit, she wholeheartedly trusted in God and His ways. She knew that He was her Creator and that He loved her as only the most devoted parent can love a child. In return, she promised to live her life in devotion to Him.

As was the custom, after she had received her schooling from the religious teachers, she returned home to her parents as a young girl of just twelve or thirteen. By this time she was known for her kind ways—speaking words of encouragement to others, finding a little extra food for those in need. Her parents carefully chose a future husband for her—a strong young man of God, a carpenter by trade.

The betrothed couple would spend twelve months apart until their wedding day. While the groom-to-be was constructing a synagogue in a distant town, the bride-to-be remained at home with her family, learning to care for a household and growing in her faith.

And so this girl—now a young teen nearing the age of marriage, as was common in her culture of long ago—lived out a quiet existence. Yet her average life hid an uncommon heart—a heart of remarkable obedience.

One day, busy with her usual household chores, the girl gasped with surprise when a bright being appeared to her. She began to tremble with fear.

"Don't be afraid," the being—an angel of God—reassured her. "I've been sent by God to tell you that you will give birth to a son. He will be a great King, and His kingdom will last forever."

Me? the girl wondered. *The mother of a King?* "But I am to marry Joseph," she replied. "How can I possibly give birth to a son? I'm not married yet!"

"God can do anything," the angel said. "Your son will be the Son of God."

Even though she did not understand, the girl knew that this messenger really was sent from heaven. "I am the servant of God," she replied. "I will do what He asks."

She immediately went to share this good news with her cousin, who was amazed and filled with joy. "Blessed are you among women, and blessed is the child you will bear!" her cousin exclaimed.

Blessed indeed was Mary, mother of Jesus. God had a plan for this young girl from Nazareth, a girl who lived a life of faithful obedience.

As you learn to walk in trust and to obey God and your parents, remember always that your life is special—God has a plan for *you*. ✳

* *

And this is love:
that we walk in obedience
to his commands.

2 JOHN 6

* *

Henceforth I learn that to obey is best,
And love with fear the only God, to walk
As in his presence, ever to observe
His providence, and on him sole depend.

JOHN MILTON

A Selfless Heart

*Like Jesus we belong to the world, living not for ourselves
but for others. The joy of the Lord is our strength.*

MOTHER TERESA

ORE MISSIONARY stories,
please!" The young girl's eyes lit up
every time she heard these riveting
tales of people serving in faraway
lands. She dreamed of a life overseas,
attending to the needs of others,
going where God's hand directed her.

Raised in the Catholic faith by her
parents, her world was jolted when her
father died. The girl was just seven
years old at the time, but her mother
continued to care for her and her three
older siblings, grounding the children
in their faith and satisfying as best she
could her young daughter's seemingly
unquenchable thirst for missionary
tales. The girl became a wealth of
information about missions, knowl-
edgeable about the different kinds of
help offered at different sites and able
to point to specific missionary stations
on the world map. She could hardly
wait to become an adult and find her
place in the world of service.

As soon as she turned eighteen,
the girl left home to become a nun.
She joined an Irish order, a commu-
nity known for their missionary work
in India. She arrived in Calcutta as a
schoolteacher, giving lessons in geog-
raphy and catechism at a local high
school and eventually becoming the

Give yourself fully to God.
He will use you to accomplish
great things on the condition that
you believe much more in His love
than in your own weakness.

MOTHER TERESA

I tell you the truth, whatever you did for one of the least of these brothers of mine, you did for me.

MATTHEW 25:40

school principal. But one day she became terribly ill and had to resign her position.

While she was recovering from illness, she heard God's call yet another time. *Leave the convent and go work with the poor. Live among them.*

And so she ventured out into the slums to teach the children of the poor, children everyone else said didn't deserve to be educated. She learned a little about medicine and began going into the homes of the sick to treat them. When she discovered that seriously ill people were living on the streets—people who had been rejected by the hospitals—she and several other volunteers scraped together enough money to rent a small space to care for them.

Soon many more nuns had joined her order. The pace at which it grew was astounding, a true testament to the selfless heart of the young girl who had dreamed of such a life. Eventually, more than four thousand nuns worldwide were running orphanages, caring for the poor and homeless, tending to the needs of the crippled and the blind.

As time went on, she received many prizes for her work, but she remained dedicated to serving the poorest of the poor. "Earthly rewards are only important if they help me to help others," she insisted. For almost fifty years, she devoted her life to being the hands of Jesus to the poor, the dying, and the unwanted.

Called by God from an early age, Mother Teresa never faltered in her service to Him. By selflessly serving "the least of these," she spread the love of Christ to a supremely needy world. God had a plan for this young girl who dreamed of tending to the needs of others in faraway lands.

As you share God's love with others, you'll be reminded that God has a plan for you. ✳

✳✳✳✳✳✳✳✳✳✳✳✳✳✳✳✳✳✳✳✳✳✳✳✳✳✳✳✳✳✳✳✳

*S*peak tenderly to them.
Let there be kindness in your face,
in your eyes, in your smile,
in the warmth of your greeting.
Always have a cheerful smile.
Don't only give your care,
but give your heart as well.

MOTHER TERESA

✳✳✳✳✳✳✳✳✳✳✳✳✳✳✳✳✳✳✳✳✳✳✳✳✳✳✳✳✳✳✳✳

So deep in my soul the still prayer of devotion,
Unheard by the world, rises silent to Thee.

THOMAS MOORE

A Dedicated Heart

Her children will arise and call her blessed;
her husband also, and he praises her.

PROVERBS 31:28

WHATEVER WILL WE DO? the young mother thought as she watched her family's home going up in flames. She hugged her little son closer to her breast—this dear little five-year-old, whom she'd come so near to losing. Standing safely outside the burning house with the rest of their children, she and her husband had heard his cries for help, but going back inside to rescue him would have been too dangerous. The flames were too hot, the smoke too thick. And so they had prayed.

Then—a miracle! The little boy appeared at the window, just in time to be snatched to safety before the roof caved in. As the mother held him, she vowed to be more careful with this child. Truly, God had saved him for a purpose.

And her own purpose? Sometimes that question was difficult to ponder. She thought back to her own girl-hood, to her devoted parents, who kept a comfortable home in a good part of town. Plenty of food, plenty of affection, and—best of all—plenty of books. How different her life was now! This was the second time the family had lost their home to fire. And her husband, careless with money, was often away from home—either on business or, worse yet, in prison because he could not pay his debts.

Yet she held fast to the ideals of her childhood. Despite being the youngest of twenty-five children, she received special attention from her father, a brilliant man who taught his daughter to think for herself. She'd often stood at the door of his study, listening to the lively conversation of her book-loving father and his friends.

Now she was a parent herself, responsible for the care of her own brood. She'd given birth nineteen times and, sadly, many of her little ones had not lived past infancy. She herself was often ill, but she dedicated herself to caring for her children in the best way possible. And so she began to teach them, using textbooks she wrote herself.

On the day following each child's fifth birthday, his or her schooling began. Despite having few resources at her disposal, she set up a little schoolroom in the house and taught her children everything from the alphabet to Latin and Greek and the classical studies of the day. The most important subject in her little school, however, was the study of God's Word. Her life was busy, but she always set aside an early morning hour for her own Scripture reading and prayer.

Her husband, realizing the great effort his wife put into training their children and developing their character, once wrote to the children: "You know what you owe to one of the best of mothers... above all (for) the wholesome and sweet motherly advice and counsel which she has often given you to fear God..."

Although she never preached a sermon in a church building or published a book or started a church, God had a plan for Susanna Wesley. Her sons Charles and John—the little five-year-old plucked from the flames as his mother prayed—founded the Methodist Church and guided tens of thousands of people to Christ. God had a plan for this dedicated young girl—now known as the Mother of Methodism—who learned at her father's knee and whose sons applied the teachings of their home life to their ministry.

So listen and learn like Susanna Wesley did, knowing that God has a very special plan for your life. ✳

These commandments
that I give you today
are to be upon your hearts.
Impress them on your children.
Talk about them when you
sit at your home and when
you walk along the road,
when you lie down and
when you get up.
Tie them as symbols
on your hands and
bind them
on your foreheads.
Write them on the
doorframes of your
house and on your gates.

DEUTERONOMY 6:6–9

A Devoted Heart

Now devote your heart and soul
to seeking the LORD your God.

1 CHRONICLES 22:19

STUDENTS, WE HAVE a new girl in our class today. Her name is Kay Lee. I know you will all help to make her feel welcome."

She was used to being introduced by teachers as "the new girl." And she was used to what would happen next. The students would scan the room, looking for an exotic new student from China, for if you say "Kay" and "Lee" together quickly, you'll see that it sounds Chinese. When the eyes of the classroom focused on the new girl—pretty, smiling, but *not* from another country—they grew a bit disappointed and, then quickly turned back to their familiar friends.

It was so hard to always, always be the outsider. The girl's family moved frequently, sometimes in the middle of the school year. She recalled the shock of the school in New York, with a gym bigger than the size of the entire school she'd previously attended. She had stood outside that gym on her first day, smiling at every girl who passed by, wishing for just one person to return her smile and say hello. Nobody had paid her any attention except for one glaring girl who had asked her, "Who are you laughing at?" in a cold, hard voice.

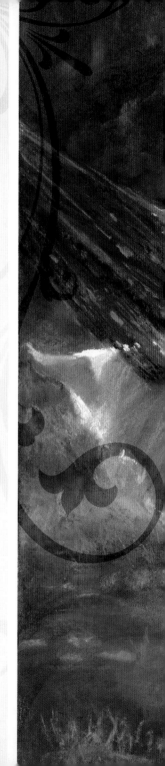

Guard my life, for I am devoted to you.
You are my God; save your servant who trusts in you.

PSALM 86:2

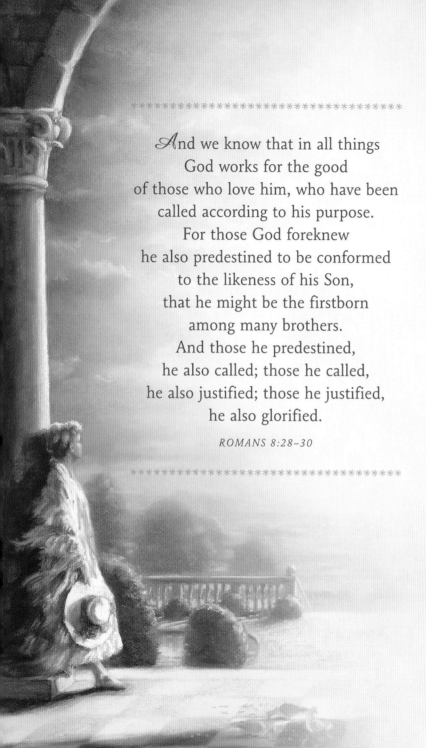

And we know that in all things
God works for the good
of those who love him, who have been
called according to his purpose.
For those God foreknew
he also predestined to be conformed
to the likeness of his Son,
that he might be the firstborn
among many brothers.
And those he predestined,
he also called; those he called,
he also justified; those he justified,
he also glorified.

ROMANS 8:28–30

New York had been a difficult move, but the girl's efforts had paid off, and she'd made several friends. Now, her parents announced that they were moving again—to Ohio, and in the middle of the school year.

The Ohio move was the worst of all. The girls there seemed to have been friends since birth, and each circle of best friends was firmly closed to outsiders. The new girl tried once again to smile and be friendly, but nothing worked. One evening, the phone rang at her house. It was for her! Maybe someone was finally calling to invite her to do something!

But the new girl's hopes were quickly dashed. An entire group of girls was calling to tell the new girl how much they disliked her, how they'd never be her friends. When her mother noticed she was crying, she got on the line to ask the group of girls why they were being so unkind. And then they began to say unkind things to her mother.

As years passed, the girl wondered if she would always know such deep loneliness in her life, if she would ever feel loved and accepted. Then, when she was twenty-nine years old, something happened that forever changed her life. She discovered that there *was* Someone who would always be her Friend, Someone who would always love and accept her regardless of who she was. That Someone was Jesus.

She learned that she could get to know God by studying His personal letter to her—the Bible—and draw closer to Him by believing His Word and His promises. She realized what it meant to truly become a Christian, to truly have a relationship with God. She basked in the comfort of His love and thanked Him for taking all the hurt she had experienced in her life and using it to make her more like Jesus. She discovered that the more she became like Jesus, the more she could love others and share the most important thing in her life with them.

God had a plan for Kay Arthur, the new girl who was rejected time and time again by her schoolmates. When she discovered God's love, she discovered that He had made her for a purpose and that He'd given her a unique passion to share what she'd learned with other women just like herself. And so she devoted her life to her Savior, writing books and Bible studies for children, teenagers, and adults—anyone longing to discover for themselves what God's Word said and how they could make it real to their lives. God called Kay Arthur, and she serves Him today as a voice of faith, encouraging this generation—in the United States and in nearly 150 countries worldwide, in 70 different languages—to know God through His Word.

The loneliness she felt as a girl inspired her to seek out others who were lonely—people who needed someone to notice them and be kind to them and tell them they were beloved of God and precious to Him. Just as Kay Arthur devoted herself to sharing God's message of hope with a hurting world, you too can reach out to others with the love of Jesus, knowing that you matter to Him and that He has a plan for your life. ✳

Kay Arthur

*Courage is not simply one of the virtues,
but the form of every virtue at the testing point.*

C.S. LEWIS

A Courageous Heart

Act with courage, and may the LORD be with those who do well.

2 CHRONICLES 19:11

"YOU'RE GOING to a new school today," Mother said. "There might be a lot of people outside there."

The bright little six-year-old nodded to her mother as she continued to dress for her first day of school. She wasn't used to new things at such a young age. She'd spent her first four years on a Mississippi farm where her grandparents were share-croppers. Her parents had worked on the farm, but it was a hard life. Her mother had been forced to carry ninety pounds of cotton on her back the day before she gave birth to the girl. Two years ago, the family moved to the city of New Orleans in search of better opportunities.

As they drove up to the school, the girl noticed the large crowd of people throwing things and shouting. *It's just like Mardi Gras*, she thought.

But it was actually far from a celebration. As the girl entered the school building, she noticed parents marching into the school and leading their white-skinned children out. She was not only the only student with black skin in the entire school—she was the *only* student in her class.

At first, she thought she had arrived early. She chose a seat in the front of the room, eager to begin her studies. When no other pupils filed in, her teacher took a seat beside her and began to teach her the alphabet. And so it continued each day for more than a year. The only student and the only teacher on the second floor of that school sat side by side, neither missing a day of class, taking their recess indoors—where it was safer for both of them—playing games and memorizing facts.

One day the teacher noticed that the girl, who usually ignored the mob that continued to shout and jeer at her, was saying something to them. "I saw your lips moving, but I couldn't hear what you were saying," she said when the girl sat down at her desk.

"I wasn't talking to them," the girl replied. "I was praying for them. Usually I pray in the car on the way to school, but this morning I forgot. When I was in the crowd, I remembered. I asked God to forgive them because they don't know what they're doing."

The family's trouble wasn't limited to the angry crowd in the schoolyard. First her father lost his job. Then the white owners of a grocery store told the family they couldn't shop there anymore. Even her sharecropper grandparents were turned off their land in Mississippi. But the family knew that this was a step they needed to take—not just for their daughter, but for all black children.

"Remember, if you get afraid, say your prayers," the girl's mother often reminded her. "You can pray to God anytime, anywhere. He always hears you." And so prayer was her blanket of protection.

Prayer and a courageous heart characterized little Ruby Bridges, who marched along, never crying nor complaining, into a school full of unfriendly faces. As the first African-American child to attend William Frantz Elementary, she paved the way for children of different races to learn and play together. Realizing that there is always a reason why we go through what we go through, she started the Ruby Bridges Foundation to promote "the values of tolerance, respect, and appreciation of all differences."

As God had a plan for courageous Ruby Bridges when she walked through that sea of hostile faces, He also has a plan for you. ❋

But Jesus immediately
said to them, "Take courage! It is I.
Don't be afraid."

MATTHEW 14:27

*We know that suffering produces
perseverance; perseverance, character;
and character, hope.*

ROMANS 5:3–4

A Determined Heart

I know your deeds, your hard work and your perseverance.

REVELATION 2:2

WALK BY NIGHT, sleep by day. Find your way through thick forests, cross deep swamps. Sometimes there's a little light, often none at all. Listen for the hounds, for footsteps, for the sound of your freedom being taken away. Always follow the Drinking Gourd. Always hope. Always pray.

The strong woman kept these thoughts in her mind as she sometimes walked, sometimes ran, concentrating on keeping one foot in front of the other despite her hunger and exhaustion. Along the route, she came upon an occasional "station"—a safe house where kind people offered food and drink and temporary shelter in a barn or outbuilding and then sent her on the next leg of the journey with embraces and prayers.

As a girl, she'd never known life to be easy. Perhaps that's why she was so determined to arrive at her destination. She knew she would face trouble along the way, but she couldn't imagine returning to the world she left behind.

Slavery had been her birthright. From the age of five, she was frequently hired out to other masters who had whipped her and treated her worse than an unwanted animal. She had been beaten even when she hadn't done anything wrong. Once she'd been an innocent observer in a dry goods store when a nasty overseer, trying to capture a runaway slave, had thrown a heavy weight in anger. The weight had hit her square in the head, and she'd suffered from blackouts ever since.

When word got to her that she was scheduled to be sold, she planned her escape that very night. She'd already endured enough separation from loved ones, enough harsh treatment from angry masters. And now she'd probably be sold down South, where unimaginable horrors awaited her. No, thank you. She'd risk everything for the promised land.

She knew she was almost there. The people at the last station had given her words of encouragement with tears in their eyes. Ninety miles she'd hiked. And then . . . the line! Freedom! She looked at her hands, sure she wasn't the same person anymore. The sun burst through the trees and over the field, shining like the golden streets of heaven. She had made it.

She knew she had a choice. She could stay here forever, basking in her newfound freedom, never having to endure another beating, never having to keep her guard up even when sleeping. Or she could return—for her parents, for her siblings, for her brothers and sisters in Christ.

Really, she knew, she didn't have a choice at all. She could never live in freedom knowing that others were still down there. And so she went back—not just one time, but twenty times, threading her way through the forests, moving silently and purposefully. Twenty trips, three hundred souls brought to freedom.

God had a plan for Harriet Tubman, conductor of the Underground Railroad and the "Moses" of her fellow African-American slaves. Blessed with an adventurous spirit and a highly determined nature, she risked her life daily as she led her people to freedom. Always confident that God would help her every step of the way, she inspired thousands to freedom.

Like Harriet Tubman, you can always put yourself in God's loving embrace, knowing that He has a plan for you. ✳

Consider it pure joy, my brothers,
whenever you face trials of many kinds,
because you know that the testing of your
faith develops perseverance.

JAMES 1:2–3

A Forgiving Heart

Be kind and compassionate to one another,
forgiving each other, just as in Christ God forgave you.

EPHESIANS 4:32

THE LITTLE GIRL tugged on her father's sleeve. "Daddy, I'm scared that I will never be strong enough to do exactly what Jesus wants me to."

The father's kind blue eyes gazed down at his small daughter. "Tell me this—when we take a train trip to the big city, when do I give you the money for the ticket? Three weeks before?"

The girl shook her head. "No, you give me the money just before we board the train."

"That's right," her father said. "That's the way it is with God's strength. God knows when you will need strength to do what is right. He will give you all you need, at just the right time."

To look at the little girl and her family, nobody could imagine how much strength they would need from God. A good-hearted man who was friends with half the city, her father owned a small jewelry store that had a constant parade of people entering and exiting its doors—sometimes for business, often for the friendly conversation they found in the shop. Her mother was known for her kindness to others.

The girl and her family were devoted followers of Christ, yet they lived and worked in the Jewish section of their

Lord, make me a channel of your peace.
Where there is hatred, let me bring love.
Where there is offense, forgiveness.

SAINT FRANCIS

city. They participated in the Jewish Sabbaths and feasts, and even studied the Old Testament with their Jewish friends, shining the light of Jesus wherever they walked.

Years later, when the Nazis invaded their country during World War II, opportunities to gain strength from God could be found every minute of every day. The family began to give shelter to their Jewish neighbors who had been driven out of their homes, working to find places for them to stay in the countryside. The girl—now a middle-aged woman—had a false wall built in her bedroom. Here she hid countless Jewish friends from the Nazis. She also used her many connections to secure ration cards that helped feed Jews hiding in homes all over the country.

Even when the family was arrested, she kept faith. Turning to Jesus time and again, she found ways to survive the prison camps. She and her sister even led worship services in the camp, using a smuggled-in Bible.

Yet despite her courage and her resourcefulness, perhaps her greatest legacy was one of forgiveness. After the war ended, she traveled the world, preaching the gospel. At one meeting, she came face to face with one of the cruelest prison camp guards she'd met.

"Please," the guard said. "I realize now that what I did was so wrong. I ask for your forgiveness."

She remembered the evil of the camp—the meager food, the backbreaking work, the harsh punishments—and felt a great struggle within. "Lord," she prayed, "I can't do this alone."

Finally, she reached out her hand to the man. As she did so, she felt a great warmth moving through her—truly, the presence of Jesus. The two stood, grasping hands for a long while. Both felt God's love melting away the past, forgiveness bringing healing.

God had a plan for Corrie ten Boom—a plan to give her strength when she needed it, strength that helped her save countless Jews from certain death. God worked in her life in every moment, from taking in Jewish friends to forgiving her captors. As you pray for God to help you in your life, you can always be comforted and know that He's made you for a purpose and He will take care of you. ✳